IT'S TIME TO EAT FUDGE

It's Time to Eat
FUDGE

Walter the Educator

Silent King Books
A WhichHead Entertainment Imprint

Copyright © 2025 by Walter the Educator

All rights reserved. No part of this book may be reproduced in any manner whatsoever without written per- mission except in the case of brief quotations embodied in critical articles and reviews.

First Printing, 2024

Disclaimer

This book is a literary work; the story is not about specific persons, locations, situations, and/or circumstances unless mentioned in a historical context. Any resemblance to real persons, locations, situations, and/or circumstances is coincidental. This book is for entertainment and informational purposes only. The author and publisher offer this information without warranties expressed or implied. No matter the grounds, neither the author nor the publisher will be accountable for any losses, injuries, or other damages caused by the reader's use of this book. The use of this book acknowledges an understanding and acceptance of this disclaimer.

It's Time to Eat FUDGE is a collectible early learning book by Walter the Educator suitable for all ages belonging to Walter the Educator's Time to Eat Book Series. Collect more books at WaltertheEducator.com

USE THE EXTRA SPACE TO TAKE NOTES AND DOCUMENT YOUR MEMORIES

FUDGE

It's time to eat, hooray, hooray!

It's Time to Eat

Fudge

A special treat comes out today.

Soft and chewy, rich and sweet,

Chocolate fudge, oh, what a treat!

Square and shiny, dark or light,

Every bite is pure delight.

Take a sniff, oh, what a smell!

Chocolate magic, I can tell!

Pick it up and take a chew,

Sticky, creamy, smooth all through.

Melts so slowly on my tongue,

Fudge is fun for old and young!

Some like walnuts in their bite,

Some like caramel, what a sight!

Plain or fancy, big or small,

I just love them, one and all!

It's Time to Eat Fudge

Mom made fudge with lots of care,

Dad says, "Wait! Let's sit and share."

Sister's grinning, brother too,

We all want a piece (or two)!

Little squares all on my plate,

Eat them fast? No, I will wait.

One by one, I take my time,

Every bite is just divine!

Oh no! My piece is nearly gone,

I've been chewing all day long!

Should I have just one bite more?

Maybe two or maybe four?

Fudge is yummy, fudge is fun,

A treat to share with everyone.

At a party, late at night,

It's Time to Eat

Fudge

Fudge just makes the world feel right!

Now my belly's full and tight,

I feel happy, pure delight.

Thank you, fudge, so sweet and true,

I can't wait to taste more soon!

Time for bed, the stars shine bright,

Dreams of fudge all through the night.

Tomorrow's snack? Oh yes, indeed,

It's Time to Eat

Fudge

More chocolate fudge is what I need!

ABOUT THE CREATOR

Walter the Educator is one of the pseudonyms for Walter Anderson. Formally educated in Chemistry, Business, and Education, he is an educator, an author, a diverse entrepreneur, and he is the son of a disabled war veteran. "Walter the Educator" shares his time between educating and creating. He holds interests and owns several creative projects that entertain, enlighten, enhance, and educate, hoping to inspire and motivate you. Follow, find new works, and stay up to date with Walter the Educator™

at WaltertheEducator.com

www.ingramcontent.com/pod-product-compliance
Lightning Source LLC
LaVergne TN
LVHW010622070526
838199LV00063BA/5248